# Pinkalicious

## Cherry Blossom

To Catherine

—V.K.

The author gratefully acknowledges the artistic and
editorial contributions of Robert Masheris and Natalie Engel.

I Can Read Book® is a trademark of HarperCollins Publishers.

Pinkalicious: Cherry Blossom
Copyright © 2015 by Victoria Kann

PINKALICIOUS and all related logos and characters are trademarks of Victoria Kann.
Used with permission.

Based on the HarperCollins book *Pinkalicious*
written by Victoria Kann and Elizabeth Kann, illustrated by Victoria Kann
All rights reserved. Printed in the United States of America
No part of this book may be used or reproduced in any manner whatsoever without
written permission except in the case of brief quotations embodied in critical articles and reviews.
For information address HarperCollins Children's Books, a division of HarperCollins Publishers,
195 Broadway, New York, NY 10007.
www.icanread.com

Library of Congress catalog card number: 2014937632

ISBN 978-0-06-224593-9 (trade bdg.) —ISBN 978-0-06-224594-6 (pbk.)

16 17 18  PC/WOR  10 9 8 7
❖
First Edition

# Pinkalicious

## Cherry Blossom

by Victoria Kann

**HARPER**

*An Imprint of HarperCollinsPublishers*

I woke up one morning
and couldn't believe my nose.
I could smell it.
I could feel it!
Spring was in the air!

This could mean only one thing.
"Is it time for the
Cherry Blossom Festival?" I asked.
"Tomorrow," Mommy said.

I couldn't wait.

I loved seeing the trees

in full bloom.

It was the pinkest day of the year!

9

"I'm going to fly a kite
at the festival this year," I said.

"Do you know how to fly
a kite?" asked Peter.
I shrugged. "I can try."

I practiced all day
but had no luck at all!
I could not get
my cherry blossom kite
off the ground.

"Keep trying," Mommy said.

"Practice makes perfect."

The next day,

we skipped all the way

to the festival.

The blossoms were more

pinkatastic than ever!

I picked out a spot

to fly my kite.

"Here goes," I said.

I started to run.

15

There was a big gust of wind.

"That's it!" I yelled.

"More wind! More!"

The breeze got stronger.

Cherry blossoms

swirled around me.

"Wait!" I said.

"I can't see!"

The wind stopped blowing.

The petals stopped swirling.

I rubbed my eyes and blinked.

I looked different.

Where was I?

"Hello," said a girl.

"My name is Sakura."

"I'm Pinkalicious," I said.

"Come on," said Sakura.

"The festival is starting soon!

Can you help me hang these lanterns?"

20

Sakura picked up a lantern
with a cherry blossom on it.
"This one is like my name," she said.
"Sakura means 'cherry blossom'
in Japanese!"

22

I picked up a bright pink lantern.
"This one makes me
think of my name, too." I laughed.

Soon a parade went by.

There were drums.

There were dancers.

There were colors everywhere!

"Try some *mochi*," said Sakura.

She gave me a pink rice cake

filled with strawberry ice cream.

I couldn't believe it.

The *mochi* was almost as yummy

as a cupcake!

I looked up at the sky
and spotted kites all around.
I got a little sad.
I wished I knew how to fly one.

Sakura understood.

"Sometimes a friend can help,"

she said.

She picked up my kite.

I held the string.

We ran together.

There was a gust of wind.

Sakura let go of the kite.

It went up in the air!

"Keep running!" she called.

My legs went faster and faster.

Suddenly, I was surrounded

by a swirl of petals.

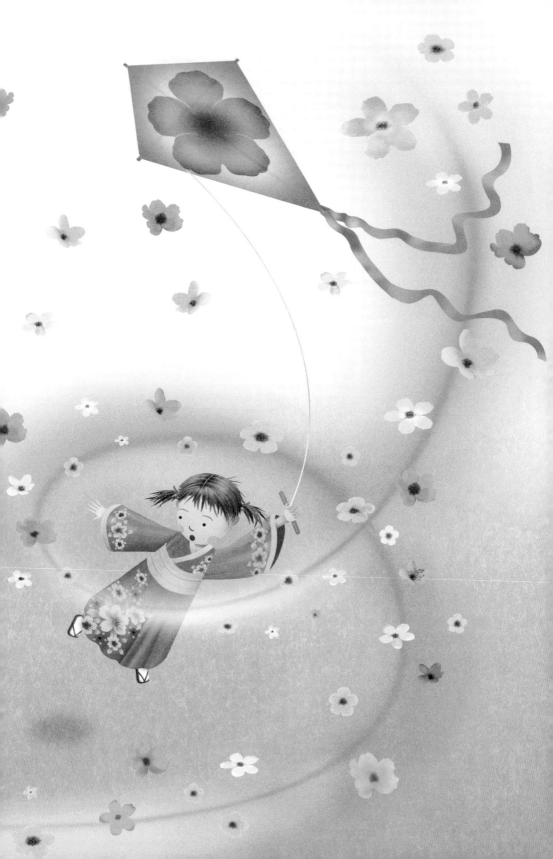

I was back in Pinkville.

My kite was still flying!

It was soaring high.

"Pinkalicious, you did it!"

Mommy and Daddy cheered.

Peter looked surprised.

"How did you get so good at this?"

he asked.

I looked at my kite and smiled.

"I got some help

from a friend," I said.

"Thank you, Sakura," I whispered.

# Dear Parent: anythink
## Your child's love of reading starts here!

Every child learns to read in a different way and at his or her own speed. Some go back and forth between reading levels and read favorite books again and again. Others read through each level in order. You can help your young reader improve and become more confident by encouraging his or her own interests and abilities. From books your child reads with you to the first books he or she reads alone, there are I Can Read Books for every stage of reading:

### SHARED READING
Basic language, word repetition, and whimsical illustrations, ideal for sharing with your emergent reader

### BEGINNING READING
Short sentences, familiar words, and simple concepts for children eager to read on their own

### READING WITH HELP
Engaging stories, longer sentences, and language play for developing readers

### READING ALONE
Complex plots, challenging vocabulary, and high-interest topics for the independent reader

### ADVANCED READING
Short paragraphs, chapters, and exciting themes for the perfect bridge to chapter books

I Can Read Books have introduced children to the joy of reading since 1957. Featuring award-winning authors and illustrators and a fabulous cast of beloved characters, I Can Read Books set the standard for beginning readers.

A lifetime of discovery begins with the magical words "I Can Read!"

*Visit www.icanread.com for information*
*on enriching your child's reading experience.*